Susanne Schaadt

Zendoodle

Meditative drawing
to calm your inner self

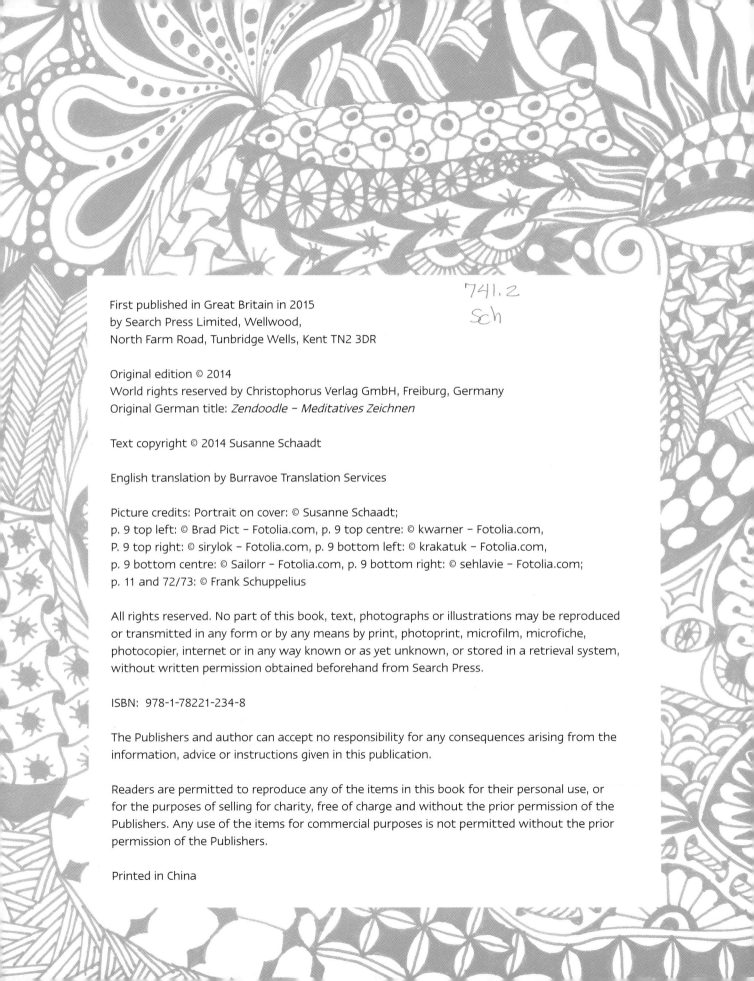

First published in Great Britain in 2015
by Search Press Limited, Wellwood,
North Farm Road, Tunbridge Wells, Kent TN2 3DR

Original edition © 2014
World rights reserved by Christophorus Verlag GmbH, Freiburg, Germany
Original German title: *Zendoodle – Meditatives Zeichnen*

Text copyright © 2014 Susanne Schaadt

English translation by Burravoe Translation Services

Picture credits: Portrait on cover: © Susanne Schaadt;
p. 9 top left: © Brad Pict – Fotolia.com, p. 9 top centre: © kwarner – Fotolia.com,
P. 9 top right: © sirylok – Fotolia.com, p. 9 bottom left: © krakatuk – Fotolia.com,
p. 9 bottom centre: © Sailorr – Fotolia.com, p. 9 bottom right: © sehlavie – Fotolia.com;
p. 11 and 72/73: © Frank Schuppelius

ISBN: 978-1-78221-234-8

The Publishers and author can accept no responsibility for any consequences arising from the
information, advice or instructions given in this publication.

Readers are permitted to reproduce any of the items in this book for their personal use, or
for the purposes of selling for charity, free of charge and without the prior permission of the
Publishers. Any use of the items for commercial purposes is not permitted without the prior
permission of the Publishers.

Printed in China

Contents

Introduction

Dear reader,

All you need is a pen and a piece of paper in order to slip into the soothing world of "zendoodle". The meditative process of drawing these intricate and imaginative patterns will allow you to escape from daily life wherever you are and whenever you like – if only for a short time. And, almost incidentally, you will create miniature works of art – regardless of whether you think you can draw or not!

It's a fact that more and more of us lead hectic and highly stressful lives and our senses can be in a constant state of over-stimulation. It can become difficult to take time out to relax, to find new energy or to concentrate exclusively on one thing. With such busy lives, it's no wonder that many people find it almost impossible to include any kind of relaxation ritual in their daily schedules.

As a relaxation therapist and artist, I am aware that many traditional methods of relaxation need to be practised for some time before you can expect the maximum benefit for the body and mind. This is why I have been absolutely delighted by the effects of drawing zendoodles. To me, they are a brilliant combination of two important things: the joy we derive from creating something, and relaxation. Then there is the tremendous positive and motivating potential that working on a zendoodle offers. There simply is no right or wrong way of doing it; anyone who can draw a line on a piece of paper can draw a zendoodle.

Children and adults of all ages have learnt this meditative kind of drawing on my course with tremendous pleasure and success. I am convinced that you will do so, too. Almost automatically, you will find you simply switch off your daily thoughts as you focus on drawing the individual lines, and often note – with amazement – how these simple lines and strokes can create a pretty pattern.

Doodle your way the new, relaxed you!

Yours,

Meditative drawing

What is zendoodle?

So where does the name "zendoodle" come from? It is a combination of the two words "zen" and "doodle". "Zen" means calming the spirit and our thoughts, finding the core of ourselves and becoming centred again. Sometimes you also find the word "meditation" used to explain "zen". "Doodle", as you probably know, just means drawing or scribbling – something many of us do, for instance, when chatting on the phone. So essentially, "zendoodle" is a calming kind of scribbling, hence the phrase "meditative drawing". The spirit relaxes as we focus on drawing simple and repetitive patterns.

The effects of meditative drawing

With zendoodling, the strokes and lines we draw are constantly repeated in a particular sequence. This results in complex patterns. Concentrating on the rhythmic setting of one stroke or line after another, and the repeating patterns, helps us to let go of our thoughts or concerns. The mind comes to rest, as it does when meditating. We start to feel an inner peace and a soothing being-at-one-ness. As we enter a state of deep relaxation, we are able to find new strength – just try it and see!
The lines that we draw carefully and steadily, and in particular the resulting patterns, will help you to find the kind of inner peace that can also be found, for instance, when drawing mandalas or perhaps when repeating a sequence of relaxation exercises. These techniques help us to find inner order – you could say that "everything is put back where it belongs". This happens automatically, quite unconsciously and with no effort whatsoever. As you draw, notice how quickly you achieve a lightness and your mood becomes more positive. At the same time, drawing helps to boost the concentration; external distractions become less important.
In addition to the relaxing aspect of zendoodling, I have also always found that the participants develop a tremendous fascination and enthusiasm for the decorative patterns and ornaments that are created as they draw. I, personally, have always had a preference for all kinds of patterns and ornaments, and have often used them in my pictures, especially large mandalas.

The fascination with patterns

Repeated, often abstract patterns are called ornaments and they can be found in every culture and age. It is almost a compulsion with us to decorate our lives with ornaments and patterns, from a simple jug to the most beautiful cathedral window. Particularly beautiful ornaments can be found in Islamic, Moorish or Celtic art as well as in Art Nouveau.

It is interesting, for example, to look at the works of Heinrich Vogeler or the intricate patterns in the Book of Kells. The ordered and regular decorations, based on the principle of repetition of the basic pattern, are not only calming and create order, but also kindle positive and pleasant feelings within us.

We can also find endless patterns and ornaments in our daily surroundings. Cast irons railings and gates, fabric patterns, tyre tracks in the snow, plants, the patterns in an animal's fur, knitting patterns, tree trunks, tiles and parquet floors are just some examples.

Tip: Be mindful as you move around your environment, and see what patterns and shapes it contains!

Possible uses

Meditative drawing is ideal for use in schools or therapy. As well as having a relaxing effect, the precise drawing and step-by-step sequences help to develop children's ability to concentrate and their attention span. Their fine motor skills and hand/eye-coordination are developed in this way, as well as helping memory performance. A zendoodle can be drawn by one person alone or as a group effort. The individual steps of the pattern are first demonstrated on the blackboard, and then the children copy them onto their paper. As the levels of difficulty of the various patterns are all different, it is easy to choose ones that suit the children's abilities and skills, so it is easy to differentiate.

Meditative drawing is also an excellent way to calm a class of children down. If only one or two patterns are explained, then the exercise will only take a few minutes and can be used as a short break in a lesson. At home, it is a good idea to get up early together in the morning and spend some time working on a zendoodle before school starts.

Every day a new pattern is explained or a version added. Of course, zendoodling and all the options it offers also make it ideal for art lessons.

It is easy to make worksheets that the children can then use to create and draw their own patterns.

Stars make an excellent group project. Eight children work together to create an eight-pointed star (see page 63). Each child fills a point of the star with a pattern, and at the end the points are glued together to create stars.

It has been my experience as an educational therapist that children love drawing these patterns. They often use the patterns I provide as the base for creating their own patterns. The method is suitable for children from about 7 years of age.

Tip: The templates at the end of the book are perfect for using in classrooms!

Pen and paper – and you can get started!

Zendoodling is a lovely leisure activity whether you do it on your own, with a friend or in a group. No preparation is required. All you need is a pen and a sheet of paper.

As the main focus is on the drawing, there are no specific techniques – the main thing is that the pen should leave a line on the paper. Over time, you may develop a preference for the tools that you work with. My favourite is a black **Fineliner** 0.4 mm on 120 or 160 g/m² white **copying paper**.

Tip: You can use a notepad or book, instead of working on loose sheets of paper.

Black ink creates a lovely contrast against the white background of the paper, and the patterns will be clear and bright. Larger areas can be blackened in a thicker felt pen.
Pencilled zendoodles are softer and gentler.
The shades of grey of a soft **pencil** (grade B) can be used for shading, to create spatial effects.
Watercolour **crayons** and **paints** and coloured **Fineliners** are all good for colouring. If the drawing is to be coloured in **watercolour paints**, use a **waterproof Fineliner** first and perhaps work on smooth watercolour paper. For really pretty effects, colour the background before drawing the patterns.

Drawing a zendoodle

There are different ways of drawing a zendoodle. The simplest method, and one that you can use anywhere, is to draw a few lines crossing each other on a piece of paper, and then colour in various patterns between the lines. The lines can all meet at a particular point, as seen in our example 1, or cross each other as in example 2. A circle or oval makes a good closed shape (example 3). Either draw the shape freehand or use a template, which you can easily make with a cup or glass. Draw lines crossing each other inside the closed shape, and then colour in these areas in various patterns. When you start, make sure that the areas are big enough for you to fill with patterns. Over time, you will develop a feeling for the right size of pattern. Patterns that are too small lose something of their pretty effect. Another design option is to fill ready-made shapes, such as a butterfly, a landscape or another motif, with the patterns at the end of the book. You will also find various other suggestions there.

Example 1

Tip: Draw when you're out and about, perhaps when you're waiting for the bus or train.

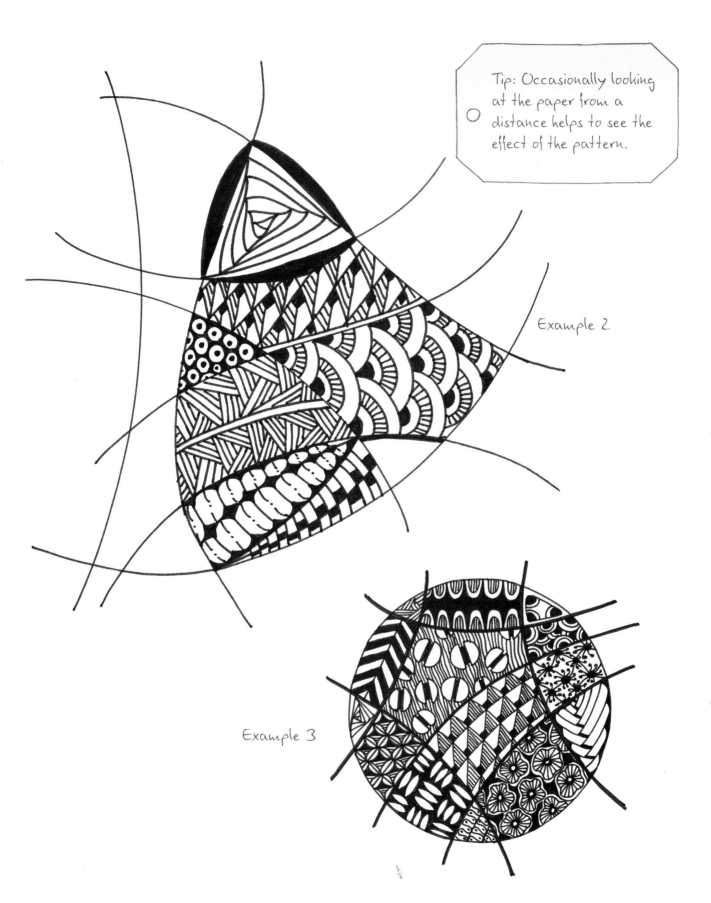

Tip: Occasionally looking at the paper from a distance helps to see the effect of the pattern.

Example 2

Example 3

The basic patterns – step-by-step

The following instructions explain, step-by-step, how a pattern is built up. The red lines or areas indicate the lines that are added in a new step. The following patterns are divided into various groups: area patterns, leaf patterns, geometric patterns, scatter patterns band patterns and single motifs.

As well as the step-by-step drawings, there are also pictures showing one version of the finished pattern: the pattern was either drawn in colour, or perhaps has been extended a little or otherwise changed. For the coloured patterns, the free areas were either drawn in colour or the patterns were drawn onto coloured backgrounds prepared with pencils or watercolours beforehand. With some patterns, a spatial effect was achieved by shading the pattern with a soft pencil.

All of these examples might help to encourage you to create your own designs. Give free rein to your imagination, and create your patterns freely and spontaneously.

Area patterns

As the name implies, area patterns fill an entire area.
They often include patterns that are based on squares.
Area patterns can be increased as much as you like, and are equally suitable for small, large and very large areas.
There are lots of different area patterns in nature as well as in our daily surroundings, and these can be used to help us create new patterns: just think of the patterns of parquet flooring, a paved courtyard, an oriental carpet or pretty fabrics. Of particular interest are the wallpapers and fabrics of the 1970s, which have recently come back into fashion.

Mountain and valley

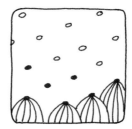

Sun hat

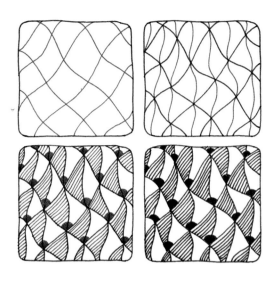

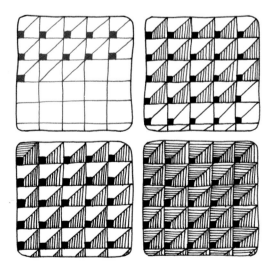

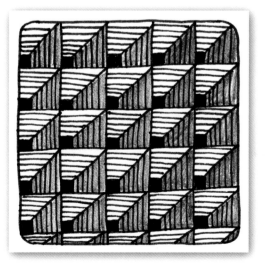

Granada

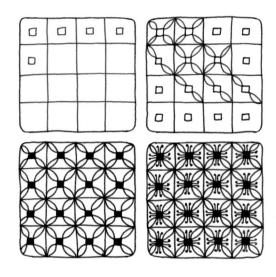

Capri

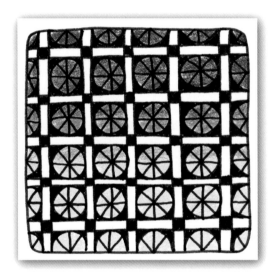

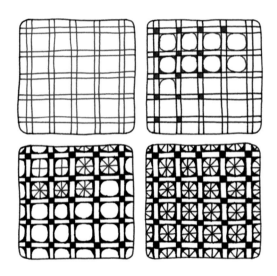

Fire glow

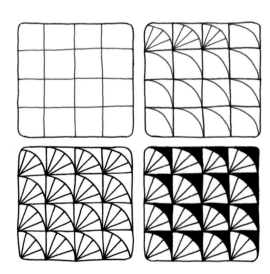

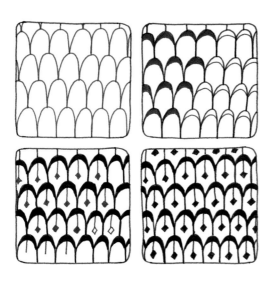

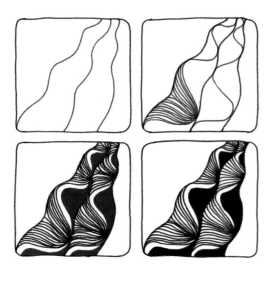

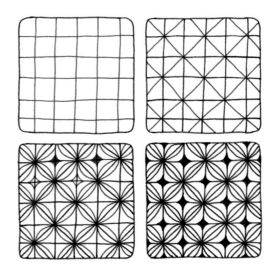

Tiles

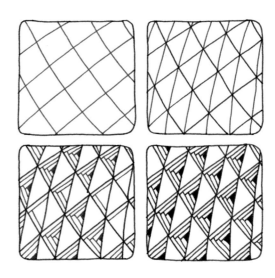

Skyline

Tangle

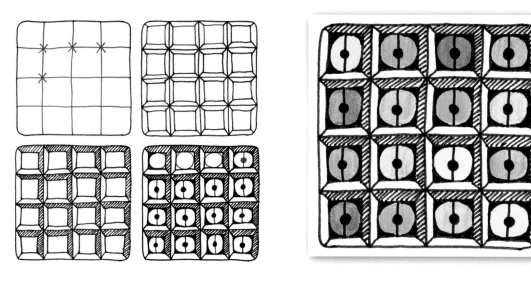

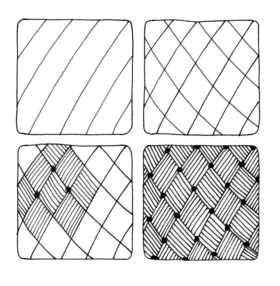

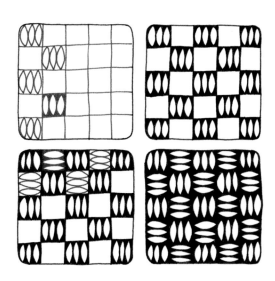

Maze

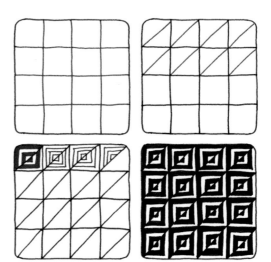

Dragon

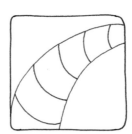

Waves

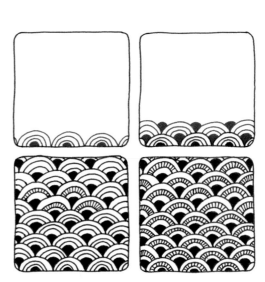

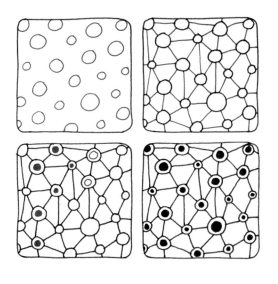
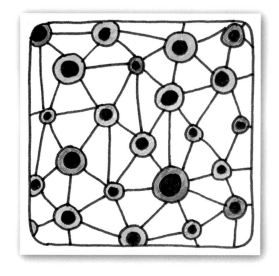

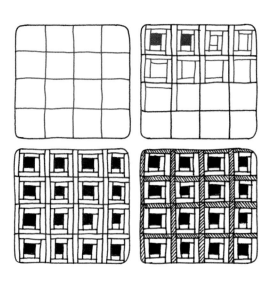

Tendril

Harmony

Checks

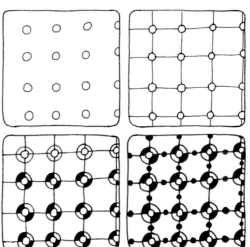

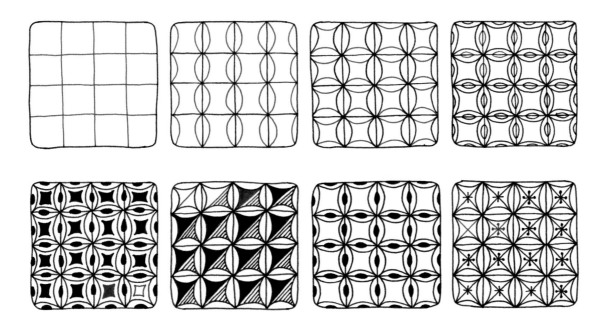

Pretty practice: Leaf patterns

Leaf patterns are based on leaves which have a slightly oval shape. As with the area patterns, a whole area is created, but in a pointed oval rather than a square shape.

You can adapt your exisiting patterns to this shape: make the little patterns on the tapered sides of the oval narrower or smaller (see below). The branch template is a lovely way to get some practice drawing various leaf patterns. It doesn't take long to draw a branch, and it creates a particularly pretty effect on writing paper or an envelope.

It can be used to decorate a pretty box that you can then use to keep dried leaves and other items from nature in.

These leaf patterns can be used in any other zendoodle.

Tip: You could use chestnut or maple leaves as your template, as they both have really interesting outlines.

Geometric patterns

Lots of people are fascinated by the effects of geometric patterns. The more precisely and evenly they are drawn, the prettier they look. Geometric patterns are basically all the same in technique, so just be brave – it's not as difficult as it looks!
You start at the bottom left. Draw a line to the next corner, stop just beside the corner, and leave a little gap. You then move to the next corner. Again, stop just beside the corner rather than at it. Continue like this, drawing from the outside to the inside in steps. The red arrows in the step-by-step drawings show you the way.

Tip: These geometric patterns are also drawn freehand; there is no need to use a ruler.

Basic triangle

The patterns look most harmonious in an equilateral triangle. But you can also play with the charming alternatives and use irregular triangles!

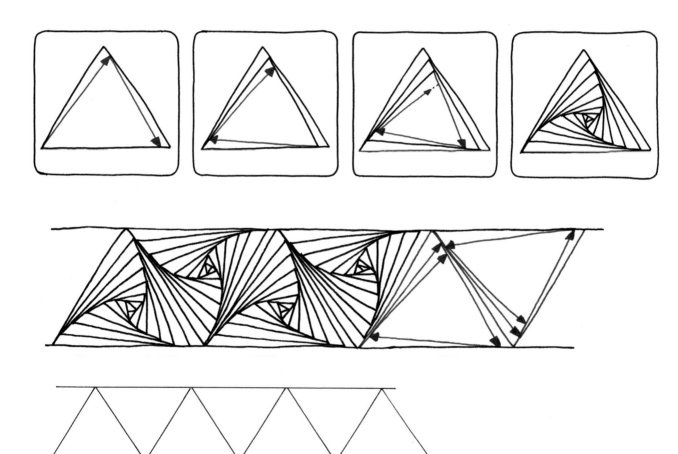

These layered patterns are created by starting the individual basic patterns at different places. Start at the bottom left corner and draw in a clockwise direction. Alternatively, start at the top left corner and continue anti-clockwise. Experiment with a number of different versions.

Try using some storytelling and creativity to help children follow these instructions:

Imagine you want to take your pencil from one corner to the next, but there's a strong wind blowing from one side and you're pushed off course a little, and end up slightly next to the corner.

Now try to get to the next corner. But there's a strong wind blowing there as well, and again you're blown slightly off-course, like before. This keeps happening, until finally you end up in the middle.

The idea is toillustrate how simply starting the same pattern in a different place can achieve different effects. There are no limits to creativity when experimenting.

Basic square

Simply arranging squares on top of and beside each other creates some very interesting layered patterns. Of course, you can also use a rectangle, and then group them together in different ways.

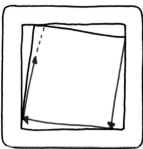 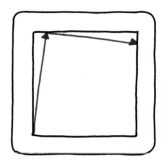 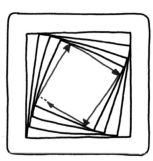 

If you're not quite so confident about drawing squares and rectangles freehand, you can use a ruler. The actual pattern is then drawn freehand. Again, you can create various layered patterns, depending on which corner you start the pattern in, and whether you draw clockwise or anti-clockwise.

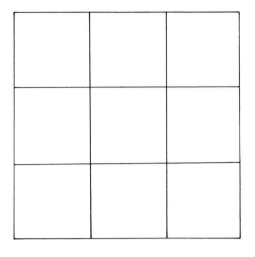

Scatter patterns

Scatter patterns are made up of lots of identical shapes that are not joined together. They are arranged over an area, either regularly or with more of them in some parts of the area. Create the individual shapes in different colours and ways. You can also colour in the background.

One illustration is enough to show many of the scatter patterns, although others are more complicated and therefore explained in several steps. Again, the red areas indicate the next progression of lines to draw.

Rugby

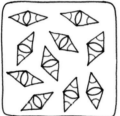

Spindle

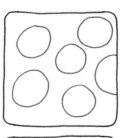
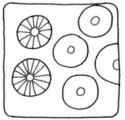

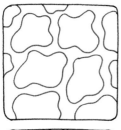
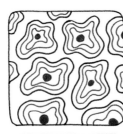

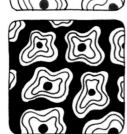
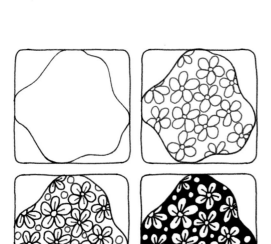

Amoeba

Wagon wheel

Marguerites

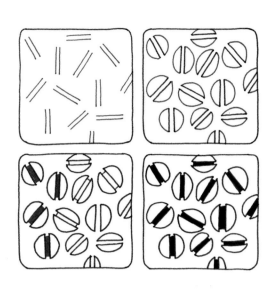

Buttercup

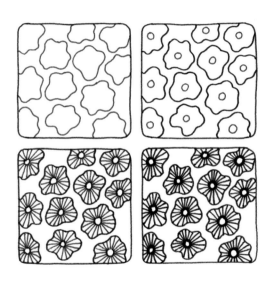

Floral magic

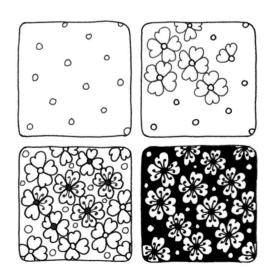

Stars

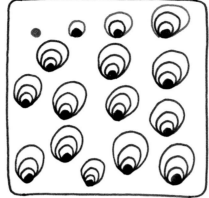

Shells

Flash

Seeds

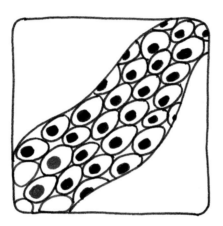

Snake

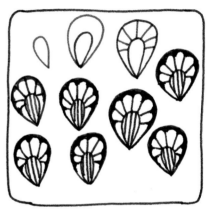

Balloons

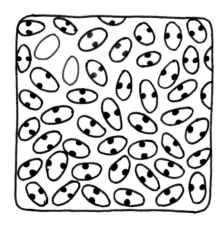

Beansprouts

Crystal

Footballs

Band patterns

Band patterns are a lovely way to make an edging or frame.
Here they are explained in the illustrations below: the red lines and areas tell you
which is the next step. Read the illustrations from left to right. The red line on the left
edge is the first line in the pattern, which is then drawn over the entire area.
Lots of band patterns can be placed together in rows or lines to fill an area – and you
have an area pattern! Usually, the band pattern runs between two parallel lines. These
lines can be straight or curvy.
Some band patterns can be drawn between two lines that are approaching each
other. Just start drawing lines on paper until you find a band that you would like to fill.

Wheels

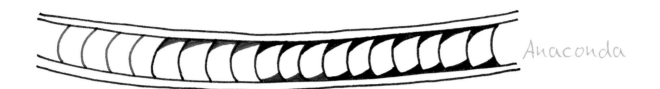

Anaconda

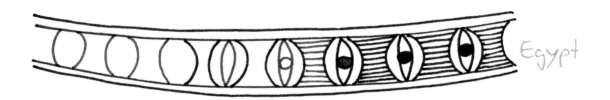

Harpoon

Egypt

Native

Woodstock

37

Target

Zip

Caterpillar

Rope

Lemon slices

Frieze

Semi-circle

Strand

Clockwork

Sunrise

Peas

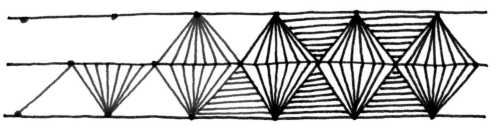

Diamond

39

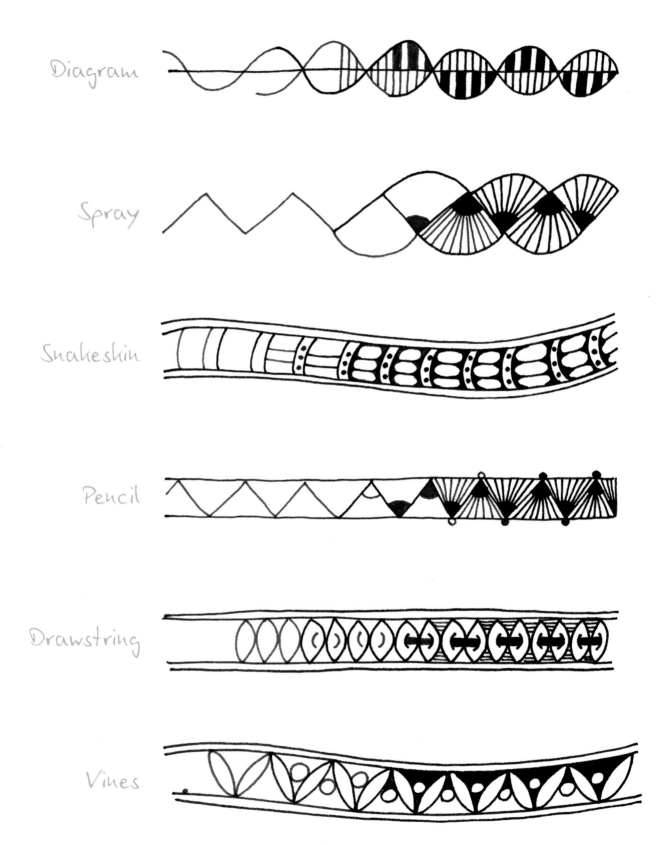

Diagram

Spray

Snakeskin

Pencil

Drawstring

Vines

40

Fountain

Border

Virtuous

Stars

Piano

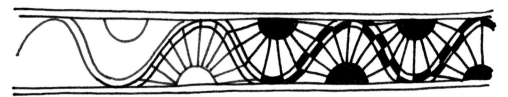

Dreamcatcher

41

Single motifs

Here are various decorative elements such as paisleys and mandalas, which can be used by themselves as single motifs or included in a big zendoodle. They make great eye-catchers!

Ornament

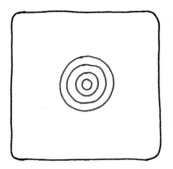   

Flower

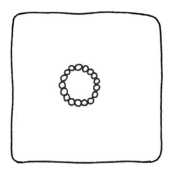   

Arch

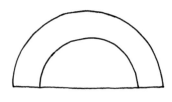   

Paisleys, flowers and little helices are all lovely as individual decorative elements. The helices look just like little snail shells. Snails, helices and ammonites are some of my favourite shapes in nature. In order to highlight the beautiful curves, it is important to use only a few patterns, and ones that adjust well to the shape.

Snail

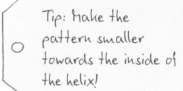

Tip: Make the pattern smaller towards the inside of the helix!

Zendoodle motifs

The motifs that follow are my favourites. You can use the templates to copy the illustrations pattern by pattern, or fill them with your own patterns, just as you like. Filling a whole motif can take several hours, but do allow yourself enough time. Of course, you can put the picture aside whenever you like, and go back to it again later on. Remember that with meditative drawing, the focus is always on relaxing and the pleasure you derive from drawing, and not on quickly achieving perfect results!

As well as the classic mandalas, stars and flowers that I show you here, you can also create patterns from landscapes or letters. The elephant and butterfly are always particularly popular on my courses!

Birds

Finely dressed in beautiful feathers, this parrot sits proudly on a branch. With lots of elongated areas, this design is ideal for band patterns. The geometric pattern of the lower beak is a little tricky, so allow yourself plenty of time for it. The area between the upper part of the face and the beak is coloured all in black. You can also use a thick felt pen in the same colour for this.

The "Tiles" pattern (page 20) looks fabulous on the parrot's wings - look out for the black outline. The branch is drawn in "Clockwork" (page 39).

This lovely little kingfisher is one of my very favourite motifs. Elegant and poised, ready for flight, he sits on a branch of plain circles. The bird is coloured in just a few patterns. When drawing the bird, it is important to make sure that the patterns follow the line of the feathers (see its body or wing). This little work of art is extremely versatile: it can be used to decorate the cover of a travel diary, cards or envelopes.

Note: See how the pattern on the beak gets smaller and smaller, finally ending in a tiny point.

Band patterns are ideal for small areas: I have used "Rope" (page 38) against a black background for the back. The tummy is "Lemon slices" (page 38), with a little additional embellishment.

Corners and edges

Pentagons and hexagons have lots of areas, which makes them ideal for experimenting with patterns.

Area patterns and band patterns are all good choices for these cornered shapes. Using larger areas filled in black and with thick dividing lines further enhances the contrast, and makes the patterns even more effective. Use a thicker felt pen for the areas and thick lines. Draw the lines slowly and with a steady hand.

Take care to draw the patterns right to the edges and into the corner, and don't let them get smaller. Trace the templates, or draw the basic shape with a ruler. The patterns are then drawn freehand.

This is what I used for the inner sections of this area pattern: "Parquet" (page 17), "Honeycomb" (page 25), "Sun hat" (page 16) and "Mystic" (page 25). I used the "Vines" band (page 40) for the fifth area, transforming it slightly and placing several bands together.

I used geometric triangles (page 28) to fill the interior of this hexagon. If that's a little too challenging, just use your favourite patterns!

The template for this motif is on page 75.

The world of plants

Blossom and flowers are good motifs for zendoodles. They are easy to draw, and the areas are generally clearly delineated. So how about decorating a nice cardboard box with zendoodle flowers?

The lotus flower on the right on page 51 shows how effective it can be not to fill all the areas with patterns. The white areas make the neighbouring ones look even clearer and more striking. As you draw, keep stopping and thinking about which parts to leave white; it's very easy to "over-draw". Area and leaf patterns are good choices for the oval flower shapes. If you're not sure about the leaf patterns, have another look at them (pages 26-27).

The frontal view of a flower shows lots of separate sections that taper at the centre. Some of my patterns are "Honeycomb" (page 25) and "Stars" (page 35). A white outline is a pretty finish to the flower.

You will find the
template for this
motif on page 76.

Fill some of the areas with scatter flowers, such
as 'Floral magic' (page 34), or just use little
dots, as seen here for the pistil. It should be as
dark as possible.
The patterns also include a few leaf patterns
(pages 26-27).

Butterfly

This one is a classic. Bright and cheerful, the butterfly flutters through the air. The black-and-white pattern of the butterfly can be coloured in with felt pens. This motif is also popular with children.

Tip: Use a waterproof pencil to draw the patterns on the butterfly. To use it as a window picture, cut it out when you have finished colouring it, and then brush it with vegetable oil. Then leave it to dry – the oil will make the paper transparent.

The butterfly's wings are more or less the same: the bottom edge is in "Vines" (page 40), and there is a triangle at the centre (page 28). The patterns along the top edge are slightly different.

Off to the Savannah

A rhinoceros is perfect for zendoodling, since the individual "armour plates" make perfect areas for filling with patterns. They all have double outlines to distinguish them more clearly.

Lots of animals make good motifs for zendoodles: crocodiles, tortoises and snails, for instance, and fish naturally have lots of areas just waiting to be filled.

Tip: Fantasy animals are also perfect for zendoodles: why not try a unicorn or a dragon!

The legs are all in different patterns!

The rhino's ears are oval, so I have used a typical leaf motif for them here (page 26). The "Pencil" band is drawn along the upper neck (page 40).

55

The soothing effect of mandalas

Mandalas are the best-known motifs for meditative drawing, and therefore perfect for zendoodling. The symmetrical construction based around a centre further enhances the calming and ordering effects of the patterns in the most delightful way. Pure meditation! In order to separate the foreground from the background more clearly, draw a thick black line over the outlines of some of the areas. In the large flower mandala (right), I have shaded the background along the edges with a soft pencil (B2) to create a spatial effect. The tree section contains a few scatter patterns. I really like the subtle colouring and the natural look of the irregular bark.

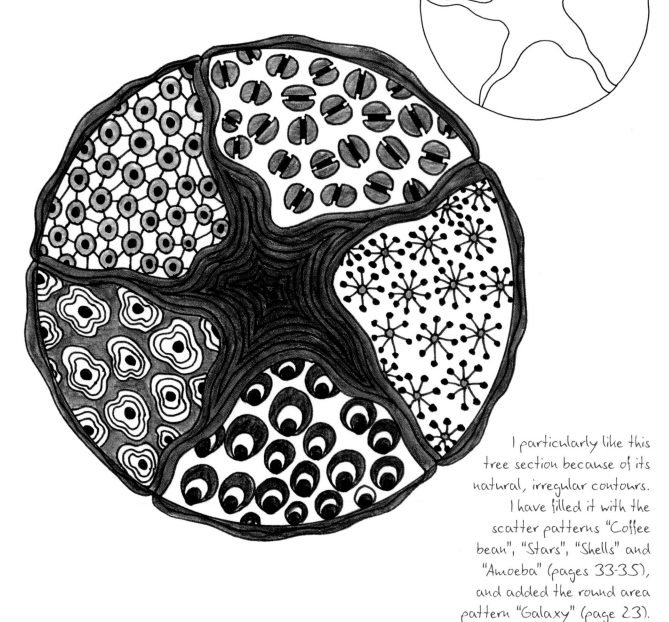

I particularly like this tree section because of its natural, irregular contours. I have filled it with the scatter patterns "Coffee bean", "Stars", "Shells" and "Amoeba" (pages 33-35), and added the round area pattern "Galaxy" (page 23).

This typical mandala has leaf patterns on the inside. I usually draw from the inside out. Here, the band "Target" (page 38) is used to decorate around the inside of the flower.

All wound up

The double helix (right) is similar in shape to the mandala. There is plenty of space for lots of different patterns on the many areas. One particular feature is the border around the helix in a band pattern. A thick black dividing line between the two helices and the narrow yellow borders between the areas clearly separate the individual patterns.

You will find the step-by-step instructions for the shells on page 43.

The "Rope" band (page 38) encloses the
outer contour of the double helix.
I have either placed bands on top of each
other for the fields, such as "Drawstring"
(page 40) or "Snakeskin" (page 40), or
I've used area patterns. The inner areas
of the helix are left white, as this shows the
surrounding patterns at their best.

Elephant

Elephants are highly revered in India, and they are beautifully decorated and adorned for special occasions. This elephant is "dressed" in lots of different patterns. I have used area patterns, band motifs and scatter patterns, for instance as on the ear. The individual decorative elements on the forehead and back blend beautifully with the overall effect. In accordance with the Indian tradition, the patterns can also be coloured in. Do not use too small a pattern for the face so that the eye and mouth can easily be seen.

Tip: If you make a mistake, just adapt the pattern slightly and work the little error into it.

Choose a single decorative element such as
"Ornament" (page 42) for the throw on the
elephant's back. It is surrounded by bands. I have
also used various bands for the legs.

Heart and stars

The heart is a combination of area and band patterns.
Subtly coloured in just three shades and shaded slightly with a
soft pencil (2B) along the edges of the bands and the outline
of the heart, it looks so spatial that you almost think you can
touch it. Why not give a very personal heart to a loved one!
With their bright colours, these irregular stars are also some
of my favourite motifs. Before drawing the patterns, I coloured
the insides of the stars with watercolours quite randomly.
I used leaf patterns for the small star. There is a geometric
pattern in the middle of the big star (page 63 bottom right).
The irregular star with eight points is a very classic motif.

Here I used the
bands "Drawstring",
"Clockwork", "Strand"
and a version of "Pea"
(pages 39 and 40).
I then filled in the
remaining fields, and
shaded along the bands
with the pencil to create
a spatial effect.

62

Here, I repeated the geometric pattern "Triangle" (page 28) in four fields.

You will find the templates for the coloured stars on page 77.

63

Letters from A to Z

Letters provide plenty of choice for designing and combining patterns and backgrounds. Both the black-and-white and the coloured letters have their own particular charm. The "E" and "K" are clear with plenty of contrasts, whether with or without a patterned edge. The "A", painted in watercolours before drawing, is cheerful and playful. The background of the angular "N" is full of patterning, and is coloured in some parts. A thick red contour and the colouring help to set the coloured letter off against the black-and-white background. Create your favourite letter or your initials with your favourite patterns. You can also make whole words or even a quote with patterns. Be sure to make the areas of the letters wide enough.

In the "E", for instance, I used the patterns "Rugby" (page 33), "Floral magic" (page 34), "Fans" (page 19) and "Fantasy" (page 23).

The "A" is a good choice for showcasing band "Hawaii" (page 36). Don't be shy about placing two different bands together, as seen at the top right with "Native" and "Egypt" (page 37).

Tip: If you have problems drawing a nice letter by hand, just print one out on the computer.

I lightly shaded the right side of the letter "K", which lifts the letter somewhat. The letter is framed by various bands.

Letter "N" consists of a leaf pattern (page 26), the "Caterpillar" band (page 38) and a modified band pattern. Some of the patterns around the outside are "Amoeba" (page 33) and "Pencil" (page 40).

Decorative elements

There are lots of lovely rounded shapes in nature that radiate a pleasant harmony, including rounded leaves, beautifully shaped stones or drops. Paisleys are lovely decorative elements that look wonderful on writing paper, cards or boxes. Just looking at these zendoodles is almost like a meditation.

You will find the template for these three paisleys on page 74.

With this one, I deliberately left some space rather than completely colouring in the paisley. This makes it easier to see the individual patterns.

Inspired by the natural shape, I drew little flowers and softly rounded patterns here. Right in the middle is a honeycomb pattern (page 25).

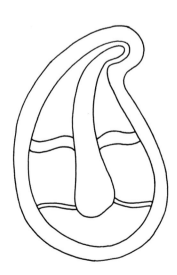

The blue colouring of the Paisley goes well with the "Waves" pattern (page 22). I drew "Vines" (page 40) all around the shape.

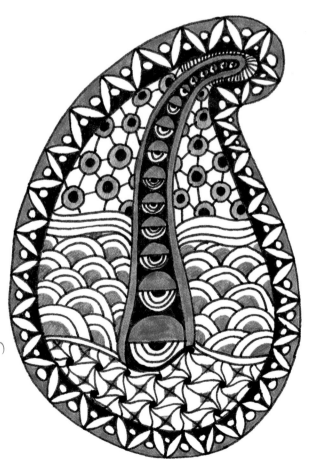

Vast landscape

Landscapes with flat hills, open fields and meadows, a meandering river or stream or steep mountains and deep valleys are lovely motifs for zendoodles, and easy to draw. You might also like a motif with a beach and the sea. Don't make the individual parts of the landscape too small – rather than drawing every individual wave or mountain peak, just simplify the silhouette.

In this landscape featuring a river, the sun's rays contain lots of the decorative band patterns, whereas I used mainly area patterns for the fields. By colouring in the zendoodle, you can instantly recognise the river and the sun. Due to the simplified structure, this landscape is also a good choice for children and teenagers.

I used lots of different patterns in this motif: the sun's rays, for instance, include the band patterns "Fountain" (page 41) top left, and the "Drawstring" (page 40) top right. I filled the sun in the area pattern "Tangle" (page 20). I used round and straight patterns for the fields.

Landmarks and architecture

Do you have a favourite city, or is there a particular landmark that is dear to you?
Then draw it – it will bring you lots of pleasure! I have chosen the world-famous "onion towers" of St. Basil's Cathedral in Moscow. Using lots of area patterns makes the spires, with the typical onion domes, look like something out of *The Arabian Nights*. As an alternative to these round shapes, you could also use a city silhouette with skyscrapers, such as the skylines of New York or Frankfurt.

Tip: With the contrast between large areas and small details (such as doors, balconies and friezes), buildings are perfect motifs for zendoodling.

I coloured the domes of the four onion towers with "Floral magic" (page 34), "Galaxy" (page 23), a simple chessboard pattern and the "Waves" pattern (page 22). You can then arrange all sorts of bands among them, horizontally and vertically!

What you can do with patterns – Examples

First and foremost, zendoodling is about the drawing, and the associated experience of pleasure and relaxation. You can often end up with lovely little works of art, almost incidentally. It would be a shame to just put them away in a drawer or folder, so what can you do with your zendoodles?

I use mine to adorn writing paper, greeting cards, bookmarks and home-made CD covers (see below for the latter two). Motifs such as the butterfly (page 53) and the star (page 63) can also be used as transparent window pictures. Just draw the patterns with a waterproof pen, then cut the motif out and brush it with vegetable oil. When dry, the paper will be transparent, and can be attached to the window. You can also use stars or mandalas to make mobiles or gift tags.

Most zendoodles can be stuck to boxes, books or pads for a really pretty effect. Paisleys and small mandalas can be used to relieve a text or as attractive decorative elements in photo albums. Individual band patterns can be stuck to strong cardboard and used to frame photos, or stuck together and used as napkin rings (see below).

Photo or picture frames can also be decorated with zendoodles. And what about some zendoodle gift wrap?

There are no limits to your imagination – or the fun to be had from experimenting!

A homemade calendar with zendoodles is sure to be a hit as a personal gift. A white or metallic pen is good for drawing on black paper or coloured cardboard, and it won't take you long to draw twelve motifs.

Of course, you can also draw the patterns directly onto an object. The glasses case (see below), which I decorated with waterproof felt pen, is one lovely example of this. However, zendoodling also works well on fabrics and textile bases: fabric shoes, T-shirts and bags can easily be individualised with fabric paints. You can also create patterns on coasters, trays and dishes – but do ask for advice from your craft shop.

A piece of furniture, perhaps a table or small chest of drawers, is certainly a bigger project, but most definitely worthwhile. For the best results, be sure to use the correct materials and tools. Your craft shop will be pleased to advise you. And beware: don't just rush into it, but take some time before you start to consider which patterns would go well on the various parts of the object!

Templates

This collection of templates over the following pages can be used as the base for your zendoodles. You can enlarge them to the size you want on a photocopier. Be sure to use 120 or 160 g/m² paper.

WELCOME

HAPPY
BIRTHDAY

Overview of patterns

Here is an overview of all the patterns, so you can easily find the ones that you would like to use for your zendoodle. The detailed step-by-step instructions for the patterns are on the pages indicated below.

Sun hat
Page 16

Centre
Page 16

Mountain & valley
Page 17

Dandelion
Page 17

Parquet
Page 17

Granada
Page 18

Capri
Page 18

Fire glow
Page 18

Blink
Page 19

Drop
Page 19

Cocoon Fans
Page 19

Tiles
Page 20

Skyline
Page 20

Tangle
Page 20

Blink
Page 21

Basket
Page 21

Lozenges
Page 21

Maze
Page 22

Dragon
Page 22

Waves
Page 22

Galaxy
Page 23

Windows
Page 23

Fantasy
Page 23

Tendril
Page 24

Harmony
Page 24

Checks
Page 24

Mystic
Page 25

Honeycomb
Page 25

Triangle
Page 28

Square
Page 30

Spindle
Page 32

Wagon wheel
Page 32

Rugby
Page 33

Amoeba
Page 33

Marguerite
Page 33

Coffee bean
Page 34

Buttercup
Page 34

Floral magic
Page 34

Stars
Page 35

Shells
Page 35

Flash
Page 35

Seeds
Page 35

Snake
Page 35

Balloon
Page 35

Beansprouts
Page 35

Crystal
Page 35

Football
Page 35

Hawaii
Page 36

Dominoes
Page 36

Corners
Page 36

Pyramids
Page 36

Wheels
Page 37

Anaconda
Page 37

Harpoon
Page 37

Egypt
Page 37

Native
Page 37

Woodstock
Page 37

Target
Page 38

Zip
Page 38

Caterpillar
Page 38

Rope
Page 38

Lemon slices
Page 38

Frieze
Page 38

Semi-circle
Page 39

Strand
Page 39

Clockwork
Page 39

Sunrise
Page 39

Pea
Page 39

Diamond
Page 39

Diagram
Page 40

Rays
Page 40

Snakeskin
Page 40

Pencil
Page 40

Drawstring
Page 40

Vines
Page 40

Fountain
Page 41

Border
Page 41

Perfection
Page 41

Stars
Page 41

Piano
Page 41

Dreamcatcher
Page 41

Ornament
Page 42

Flower
Page 42

Arch
Page 42

Snail
Page 43

Afterword

Ever since I was a child, I have been fascinated by patterns and ornamentation. There are so many beautifully created works both in fine art and in general arts and craft. The structures and patterns in nature also never fail to delight me. Even as I child, I found it quite relaxing to draw patterns. I remember automatically reaching for a pencil and drawing patterns in difficult times, knowing instinctively of its meditative and healing effects.

And quite aside from that, drawing is extremely enjoyable. I hope that I have succeeded in sharing a little of this pleasure and delightful effects with you in this book, and that you too will be enchanted by the world of patterns and ornamentation.

I have so often heard people say on my courses, "I can't draw" or "I have absolutely no talent at all, and I hardly even dare try although I would really love to". Anyone, really anyone at all, can draw using the zendoodle method, regardless of talent or gift, and can enjoy the relaxation it brings and create little works of art.

I really can't think of a better or lovelier way to create and relax at the same time. So I would like to encourage you to take up a pen and paper and just make a start.

I hope you really enjoy zendoodling, and the relaxation that it brings.

Yours,

S. Schaadt